BIG · PICTURE DICTIONARY

Illustrated by David Anstey
Written by A J Wood

CLB

Colour Library Books

A DINOSAUR FAMILY

TV aerial

Chimney

Tree

Drainpipe

Window

Door

Uncle

Grandpa

Auntie

Path

Sister

Twins

Brother

Grandma

HOME SWEET HOME

Picture

Lamp

Doctor

Banni[ster]

Patient

Book

Pet cat

Cupboard

Bed

Rug

Slippers

BEDROOM

LIVING ROOM

Curtains

Sofa

Telephone   Television

Pet dog

Stairs

Cushion

Armchair

Table

Doorma[t]

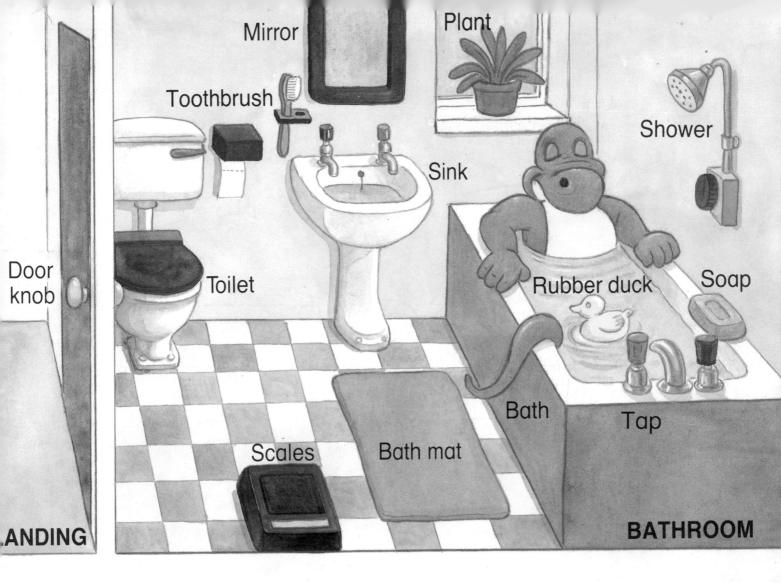

Mirror

Plant

Toothbrush

Shower

Sink

Door
knob

Rubber duck

Soap

Toilet

Bath

Tap

Scales

Bath mat

LANDING

BATHROOM

HALL

KITCHEN

Clock

Pan

Jug

Blind

Stool

Sink

Cooker

Rolling pin

Jar

Chair

Kitchen table

Cupboards

LUNCH

Paper cup

Sandwiches

Ham

Orange juice

Salad

Bread

DINNER

Fizzy drink

Salt

Dessert

Glass

Beans

Pepper

Potatoes

Sausages

Meat

Barbecue

Balloons

Paper hat

Lemonade

Sandwiches

Crisps

Biscuits

OUT SHOPPING

Apples   **Pears**

GREENGROCER   **Melons**   **Oranges**   **Bananas**

CLOTHES SHOP   **Jumpers**   **Bag**

Scarf   Hat   Coats   Boots

TOY SHOP   Jigsaws   **Books**   **Doll's house**

Tricycle   Building bricks

Train set

SUPERMARKET   **Milk**   **Cheese**

Trolley   Tins   Eggs

Lemons Potatoes Tomatoes Lettuce

Pumpkins Carrots Marrows

Briefcase Shirts Tie

Shoes Jacket

Trousers

Toys Toy plane

Rocket

Kite

Boat Robot

Ball Toy car

Cash register Packets

Fish

Bread Meat Basket

DINOSAURS AT WORK

Teacher

Pupil

Artist

Painter

Builder

Hairdresser

Musician

Carpenter

Dancer

Astronaut

Pilot

Chef

Salesman

Scientist

Mechanic

Shopkeeper

Racing driver

Soldier

Computer operator

ROUND THE YEAR

SPRING

Clouds

Rain

Daffodils

Puddle

Raincoat

Lamb

Boots

Twig

Bud

Bird

Eggs

Nest

SUMMER

Sun

Sunshade

Hammock

Swimming pool

Diving board

Rubber ring

Tennis racket

Tennis ball

Bee

Rose

AUTUMN

WINTER

ON THE FARM

Barn

Kitten

Pitchfork

Kennel

Ladder

Hay

Cow

Calf

Farmer

Tractor

Hedge

Mud

Sheep

Gate

Farmhouse

Fence

Field

Dog

Goat

Bull

Horse

Stable

Geese

Chickens

Cockerel

Sack

Dove

Pig

Pigsty

Piglets

Lamb

AT THE SEASIDE

Hang glider

Lighthouse

Buoy

Speedboat

Water skier

Rocks

Sail

Yacht

Net

Surfer

Snorkel

Swimming costume

Sunhat

Seashells

Surf board

Crab

Wave

Beachbc

Swimming trunks

Towel

Starfish

Sandcastle

Bucket and spade

Ocean liner

Tent

Cliff

Fishing rod

Flag

Fisherman

Seagulls

Flagpole

Beach ball

Beach

Lifebelt

Pebbles

Telescope

Ice cream

Windbreak

Deckchair

Oars

Rowing boat

THINGS WE DO

Laughing

Falling over

Climbing

Dancing

Diving

Drinking

Eating

Jumping

Kicking

Hiding

Shouting

Bathing

Crawling

OPPOSITES

Straight

Up

Down

Crooked

Tall

Short

Fat

Shut

Open

COLOURS

Yellow

Green

Rainbow

Grey

Orange

Pink

Black

Brown

Purple

Blue

Red

White